DISCIPLING CHILDREN FOR CHRIST THROUGH INFLUENCE

DISCIPLING CHILDREN

BOOK 1

THEODORE ANDOSEH

Published by

A division of the Book Ministry of Christian
Missionary Fellowship International

info@books4revival.com

CONTENTS

In a world where distractions abound and the allure of worldly pursuits is ever-present, the task of nurturing young hearts into disciples of Christ is more critical than ever. The message contained within these pages was delivered by Theodore Andoseh at the *World University of Prayer And Fasting* course for children aged 10–18 in Koume, from the 9th to the 11th of February 2023.

The author takes us on a curated exposé on how <u>attraction begets admiration, admiration begets imitation, and imitation begets transformation</u>. It is a journey to understand the profound impact of attraction and admiration in discipling children for Jesus.

Many may be surprised to learn that there came a time in Jesus' earthly life when He ran away from home. The questions arise: When did the Lord run away, and why? Through careful examination, we uncover that something irresistibly attracted the Lord Jesus, compelling Him to seek it out. It is in this revelation, alongside the inspirations by the lives of

Mary, John the Baptist, Timothy, and the disciples of Samuel, that we find <u>the power of attraction and admiration as mighty tools in shaping the hearts of our children for Christ.</u>

As <u>ministers to children and parents</u> alike, our mission is clear: to direct the admiration of children heavenward, guiding them toward a deep and transformative relationship with their Saviour. The stories and testimonies within these pages serve as a testament to the profound impact of nurturing admiration for the things of God in the hearts of our youth.

May this book serve as an inspiration for all who seek to become effective disciple-makers for the children entrusted to their care. Let us turn to the Bible and glean wisdom as we endeavour to raise <u>a generation of worshippers who walk with God</u> from their earliest days.

Koume, 30th January 2024

INTRODUCTION

I want twenty children to come and stand in front here. I want each one of you to tell me somebody that you admire: in your school, in your church, in your locality, or on television, somebody that you admire.

The exercise we have done is a very serious exercise. Admiration produces imitation. The exercise we have done is very serious, the person you admire, you will find it easy to imitate.

Admiration produces imitation.

Admiration produces imitation.

And imitation produces transformation.

What our children admire, they will imitate. What they imitate, they will become. What our children admire, they will imitate. What they imitate, they will become. That is because admiration produces imitation, and imitation produces transformation.

Admiration produces imitation, and imitation produces transformation.

Admiration produces imitation, and imitation produces transformation.

We ought to pray for our children and pray hard, that they will admire the right people, and be attracted to the right people

- in their age groups,
- amongst older people,
- the people in their environment,
- the personalities of their studies
- and the personalities in their entertainments.

If your child admires the wrong person, you are doomed, because admiration will produce imitation and imitation will produce transformation.

In the Bible, four ministers to children knew it. They carried their children to go and see Jesus, so that Jesus may touch them, so that the children may feel Jesus, His tenderness, His love and remember it. Many parents carried their children to go and see Jesus, so that they may love Him, so that He may bless them, so that He may touch them. They expected something from that encounter with Jesus. Even though the children may not have understood the Gospel, even though the children may not have been in need of healing, they brought the children to meet Jesus, to be touched by Jesus. This is because the ministry to children and the building of children come down to the mighty principle of attraction and admiration.

What the children admire, they will imitate; what they imitate, they will become. So, in discipling children, it is important that we offer to them icons that they can admire. If what the child remembers about the minister to children are some old women who never laugh, who always have a cane, and who use the cane very generously, we have discipled them away from the church.

When we started the training of ministers to children, in the course we had in Mokolo, one of the things I insisted on is that every minister to children should cry to God for favour, and should do everything to be liked. A minister to children's first ministry is to make themselves loved and admired; otherwise, all is lost. Admiration, imitation, transformation, that is the principle of discipling children.

If we fail in producing admiration, we have lost everything.

I want us to understand very simply and believe what we are saying. If you take your child and send on holidays to an uncle who is richer than you, who buys him a bicycle out of just simple love, that act remains in your child's mind, he will admire your uncle, not you; because you have never bought him even an ice cream. You will have shown him somebody to admire. He will admire that person and begin to absorb all that person does and values.

If a child sits down with the mother and always hears the mother regretting: "Oh, I did not finish school", the child ends up knowing that those who finish school are happy. And the mother is not happy, even though she is a believer, because she never finished school. You will have told your child not to admire you, not to be attracted to you, because you did not finish school. Your child now knows what makes people unhappy: when they do not finish school. They don't see you rejoicing in your salvation! They don't see you thanking God for His mercies! They see you always sighing!

I had a young girl that was living with me, the daughter of some missionaries. When she was very small, every time I went to their house, the parents would cook some special food. So, she knew that I was somebody very important, I was a missionary. She was eight years old. When I got home and I hugged her, she would tell me: "Uncle when I grow up, I will be a missionary-doctor". I will be a missionary like you, and I will be a doctor by schooling.

Her parents also went on the mission field, and she went with them. After some years, she came back to live with me and continued her studies. Then one day, she told me: "Uncle, you remember when I was small, I used to tell you that when I grow up, I will be a missionary-doctor. Now, I have dropped the missionary; I will be a doctor." I said: "why?" She said: "You see, I went on the mission field with my parents. Every time my father stands up to preach, he tells the church how they don't appreciate how much the missionary life has cost him, and that before he became a missionary, when he used to be a big teacher, his students appreciated him, now he comes to church and the brethren talk to him anyhow." So, the little girl told me: "My father says it over and over and over. So, I came to the conclusion that he regrets being a missionary, and that the best part of his life was when he was a big teacher. So, uncle, how can I see what has frustrated my parents and want to do it? Drop the missionary part; I will be a medical doctor." And she is a medical doctor today, and not a missionary.

By the things we admire and even by the way we talk, we are telling people what to admire. If we are always complaining, why should our children become like us? When people visit us, our children see, they see those we give attention to. They see those that we treat with importance. If we treat those who are poor very carelessly, and we are obsequious to those who have big cars, we are telling them who to admire, we are forming their values, we are offering them models.

What attracts us, we will admire. What we admire, we will imitate, and what we imitate, we will become.

If you want to summarise it, all that attracts a man is what the man will become. All that attracts a man is what that man will end up becoming, and it starts at childhood. When you buy a new dress for a child, tell them: "Thank God, because He is the one who gave us money to buy this dress. When there is food on the table, you don't just jump on the food like a pagan. You tell the child: "Sit down! Let us thank God who provides for our daily bread." Someday, that child will know that all good gifts around us are sent from heaven above, so we thank the Lord. We thank the Lord for His love. We thank the Lord and we thank the Lord for all His love... "that is how we harvested our plantain." All good gifts around us, are sent from heaven above. That is why we thanked the Lord and we thank Him, for He loves us. Where does that come from? It comes not from teaching hymns, it comes from thanking God for food on the table every day. It comes from referring the child to God, the Doer of all good. I don't mean that you tell the children to thank God; No! But that they see you thank God, and they join you to thank God, to thank God for waking up in the morning, to thank God at the end of a hard day's work. We thank God for all his good deeds.

If we teach the characters of the Bible without the goal of making them attractive, they will know the Bible stories and admire worldly musicians.

> Attraction produces admiration,
> Admiration will produce imitation,
> Imitation will produce transformation,

and we shall have made a disciple, and we shall have produced a disciple.

We have many rivals that are fighting with us. We have a lot of rivals. In the family, you may bring your wicked cousin who steals groundnuts and gives your child to eat, and then, your child admires this uncle who always gives him forbidden groundnuts. When that uncle tells him something to do, he will do it with joy, when that uncle tells him: "When you go to papa's room, check in his pocket, you will see some coins, bring them!" Your child will do it. And that is how your child will begin to be misguided. His Uncle will not plainly have told them to steal. He started simply by giving him sweets and groundnut time and again, in secret. He eventually gains the child's trust. And, right before you, another is 'taking care' of your child better than you. Some perversion in us believes that when we have given birth to a child, that child must love us automatically; so, we make no effort to be close to the child and influence him, especially the influence that captivates. And lo, some other person brings it into the life of our children. Discipleship is influence.

We have about five programmes for children each year:

- There is this course in February. And over the years, I have laboured to use it as <u>a course for the</u>

discipling of the children. We started it as a course for Headquarters' children. My burden was that if we produce some children who start very early by being disciples of Jesus Christ, they will go very far.

- In June, we labour to encourage profile children. We take those who became great leaders and then, we study how they laid the foundation of their greatness when they were children. Because if we bring our children to lay the foundations that these profiles of the Bible did, then our ministry will always have great spiritual profiles.
- In the youth camps, we want to train the children to know God and be useful to God, as they are now. We want the children to learn how to be useful to God.
- And we have the School of Knowing and serving God (SKSG) course for the profile children, our small school of prophets, where we want to produce those who walk in holiness and know God.

Last year, I shared with the children how to become champions for God, in this course. I have a burden this year. Last year, I spoke about champions; but this year, I want to speak about worshippers, children who are worshippers. It is the object of our worship that we admire and that transforms us.

The key word this year is 'worshipper'; last year, it was 'champion'. The children's version of the SKSG. It is for them to develop deep knowledge of God, to walk with God, so that God may have people that He can use, people like Mary, John the Baptist, and the others that the Lord used. And, even if God does not use them (like the disciples of Samuel), that there will always be people in CMFI who walk with God because they have done so right from childhood.

Do we know the names of all the youngsters that Samuel trained? They were still young when Samuel recruited them to build them as his disciples. He taught them to pray, he taught them music, he taught them singing, and he taught them to play musical instruments. And when they started singing and dancing, even the men who were on mission to kill fell under the power of the Holy Spirit. We do not know all their names, but we thank God that these few children gathered around Samuel. They are not profiles. However, they are people who changed the spiritual atmosphere and environment in the entire nation through their prayers, through their praise.

So, this year, for this course, we shall learn how to build our children into true disciples of the Lord Jesus-Christ, practically, from where they are, not with big words like accountability, but by observing simple principles.

1

JESUS'S ADMIRATION

INTRODUCTION

We shall study what the Lord Jesus admired; we shall consider when Jesus ran away from home. Because Jesus also ran away from home once. In His case, it was to go to the Temple because He loved the word of God. Say Amen. But when it is you, where do they find you?

I want to bring discipleship to Jesus down to the level of each of our children. You are free, equally, to run away if it is to pour yourself into the Word of God to the point of forgetting about food. When Jesus ran away, how many days did His parents search for Him? Three days!

Where did Jesus go? He went to the House of His Heavenly Father. What did He go there to do? It was not to pray, but to listen to the Word of God. He went and spent time there with some old daddies. That is why I spoke of those we admire. The people that Jesus admired were bearded men, men with white beard. It is amongst these men that He went and sat. And He asked them questions: "What did Moses mean by this? " And they explained. And He said: "It means that things were like this, like that". "And those bearded men watched Him and said: "He understands clearly! He understands very clearly! How could a child understand things so clearly?

For three days, the TV that Jesus watched was those bearded old experts in the Law. Those bearded old men were so fascinated by this little child that they did not even ask who his parents were. They did not do so because Jesus ended their boredom. Before then, they were bored! They had much knowledge, and there were not many people who wanted to listen; finally they had a fan; Jesus was the fan of those bearded men who had lenses because they studied the Bible a lot.

I spoke of what we admire because we have many rivals: the movies, worldly music, the Internet, and there are many stars like Mbappe that people admire. We want to influence the world, and we have no icons that our children admire, like the Lord Jesus who admired those who knew the Word of God.

We shall look at when Jesus ran away.

Great captivations lead to admiration.

Admiration produces imitation.

And imitation eventually transforms you.

A man puts on the person that he has admired.

THE WORD OF GOD

The Lord Jesus admired the Word of God. When He was very young, at the age of twelve, there was only one time He ran away from home, because He wanted to go and enjoy the Word of God. Many of you, run away from home to go and watch *Tom and Jerry*, *Daffy Dog*. But the Lord Jesus' *Tom and Jerry* was the Word of God: He wanted to hear the Word of God, He wanted to learn the Word of God.

There are some children, even when they are young, who love big people. The Lord Jesus was one of them. Instead of playing with his friend, He ran away from home once to go and hear the Word of God. He went and sat among them, among old, venerable, austere, long beards, picking eyes elders who had read the Bible all their lives. They did not have glasses in those days, but just imagine that they were wearing glasses, round glasses like Ghandi's glasses, perched on the tip of their nose like a headmaster, with their trousers always near their breast, listening to the Word of God.

Luke 2:41-52

*Every year his parents went to Jerusalem for the Feast of the Passover. *^{42}*When he was twelve years old, they went up to the Feast, according to the custom. *^{43}*After the Feast was over, while his parents were returning home, the boy Jesus stayed behind in Jerusalem, but they were unaware of it. *^{44}*Thinking he was in their company, they travelled on for a day. Then they began looking for him among their relatives and friends. *^{45}*When they did not find him, they went back to Jerusalem to look for him.*

^{46}After three days they found him in the temple courts, sitting among the teachers, listening to them and asking them questions.

[47]Everyone who heard him was amazed at his understanding and his answers. [48]When his parents saw him, they were astonished. His mother said to him, "Son, why have you treated us like this? Your father and I have been anxiously searching for you." [49]"Why were you searching for me?" he asked. "Didn't you know I had to be in my Father's house?" [50]But they did not understand what he was saying to them.

[51]Then he went down to Nazareth with them and was obedient to them. But his mother treasured all these things in her heart. [52]And Jesus grew in wisdom and stature, and in favour with God and men.

Jesus disappeared for how many days? and where did His parents look for him? They first thought He had gone to be with His friends; so, they inquired from them and no one had seen Him. You should notice that Jesus also had friends.

When the Lord Jesus ran away, they were in Jerusalem. Strictly speaking, He did not run away from home. They were going back home but He did not want to go back because He loved the Word of God. The parents looked for Him among His friends, they did not find Him. They looked for Him among their relatives and they did not find Him. They looked for Him among the fellow travellers back to Nazareth and they did not find Him. Then, they went to Jerusalem, looked for Him everywhere, and finally found Him in the temple, in the house of God, sitting down, not playing. When the Lord Jesus ran, He did not go to play; He sat down with elderly men, because there was a hunger in His heart. There was a tendency, a desire, an instinct for the house of God, for the presence of God and for the Word of God.

2

SPIRITUAL TENDENCIES

One of the things I keep looking for, when I relate to children, is to find their spiritual tendencies. When I hug children, when I play with them, I am desperate to discover their spiritual tendencies. Even when the Lord Jesus was young, there were great tendencies in His heart for the presence of God, for the Word of God.

What are the spiritual tendencies of each of your children?

Children, what are your spiritual tendencies? What are your spiritual tendencies?

We should study what the spiritual tendencies of our children are:

Do they like serving?
Do they like to sit down and listen?
Do they like singing?
Do they like dancing?
Do they like praying?

Do they like to go to the places where people are praying?
Do they like giving?
Are they kind?
Do they like making peace?

You see, when some small children find another child that is angry, they will just say "Go away!" But there are some children who will like to make the person who is angry to calm down.

As you watch the children, what are their spiritual tendencies? What do you catch them doing on their own that has eternal flavour? What do you catch your children doing on their own, that has eternal flavour?

There are children who are curious, there are children who like to fight, there are children who like to talk, they talk until they look like a clock always moving, and there are children who talk, talk, talk, who play, play, play, and there are children who are destructive. Who has watched a child who is destructive? If he sees something which is good, he just wants to spoil it. He always wants to spoil something. And there are children who are mischievous.

In all the tendencies of your children as you watch them, what have you noticed that has heavenly flavour?

The Lord Jesus had those tendencies:

- A hunger for God's presence
- A desire to be in the temple
- An enjoyment of hearing the Word of God

We should notice the spiritual tendencies of our children, especially after they say that they have believed. What are your spiritual tendencies?

For the Lord Jesus, it was to be in the presence of God. He had spiritual intelligence which the old people admired, from the questions He asked, the answers that He gave when they asked Him questions. In the building of children, we should craft their interests, we should figure out what they are interested in.

One young man wrote to me from Ngaoundéré. He told me: Brother Theodore, I have gone to do engineering, since it is something, I love so much, I went and did computer engineering, so that I may never work for the rest of my life, because when you do what you like, you do not work; it is what you enjoy.

If we succeed to channel the children's affections to heavenly things, they will never be religious; they will love God. Even for those who are bigger, the Bible says "Set your minds on things above" (Col 3:2) Thus, there will be no efforts being religious. When you do what you enjoy, you do not feel the work; you are not working.

If we craft the interest of our children from when they are young, they will never be religious because they will love God. The man who loves God cannot be religious, because he loves God. But if when the children are young, we gave them to love the world, we allow them to love the world, we do not craft their affections and they follow their friends to love their friends' love. You can buy them a laptop and they follow everything that is in the laptop, they love what is in the world; and, later on, you tell them to meditate, they will open the book and do nothing because the whole mind is blocked towards God. Then as soon as you put a cartoon, they start explaining to you everything, because they know everything.

I sat down with one young boy for four hours in Kinshasa, in the house where we were lodged. There was a cartoon movie on the screen in which I did not understand anything, but the boy was enjoying it. So, I asked him: « Sonny, do you understand it?" He replied: "Yes, Grandpa! That animal seeks to hide. "I asked him, "Which animal?" He should have asked himself: "How can this old man be so stupid?" I did not even see the animal, I saw lines, pictures, things just popping up left and right, motion. I understood nothing; he understood everything, he followed the story perfectly.

It is on that day that I knew that if we miss cartoons, we may not communicate. Cartoons are not stories, but a language like pidgin. And there are those who understand nothing like me! Do you understand cartoons? On that day in Kinshasa, I promised to do everything possible so that we develop animated films. The kid was about seven. He watched TV continuously for four hours. He was focused, he did not go out to play. Cartoons are a language, children's mother tongue. Say Amen! We must preach the Gospel to the children in their language.

I was bored; I understood nothing. The boy was tired of explaining to me. If he wasted more time trying to help me understand, he would miss something; so, he simply let me be. I am not pretending: I understood nothing, I only saw things moving up and down on the screen. I will sleep if you show me an animated film for 15 minutes.

*Pray that we will help children develop their inter-
est, healthy interests.*

It will hook them to eternal pleasures, they will never be religious, because they will love God. If we don't, then all that
we are giving to them is external, because inside, there will
be other things that interest them.

That was just an example, what I am drawing attention to is
that Jesus had that which attracted Him, and that which
made Him go outside discipline in order to go and enjoy.
Jesus had that which gave Him enjoyment. There were the
tendencies of His heart. In the Bible passage we read, for
once, Jesus did not behave as he should, because He was
attracted to those things His heart wanted.

Now, you, our child, what are the things that your heart
craves, especially since the day you claim to have believed?
Since then, what are the attractions of your heart? What do
you enjoy doing for the Lord, for which you need no orders?
Who have you surprised by singing a hymn ? Who will catch
you reading your Bible? Who will catch you watching something heavenward? Jesus had heart impulses.

I am not preaching so that we produce cartoons. My point is:
have you noticed the spiritual impulses of the children you
have been with? What are your spiritual impulses? What do
you enjoy doing? if there was nothing called accountability,
what would people catch you doing? What are your spiritual
inclinations? We have said that the impulse of the Lord Jesus
Christ was to go to the presence of God, to hear the Word of
God, to be where there is the Name of God, to be in the
house of God. What about you?

We are teaching a lot of things to our children, a lot of doctrine. We shout at them and tell them how good children behave. Who told you that they want to be good children? We are just taking things for granted. When did they tell you that they wanted to be good? Consider the people whose presence they enjoy, the uncles, the aunties, and the others; are they good people? Are they not thieves who give them sweets? Are their friends at school good people? Is it not the mavericks that they admire? Those who can talk, troublemakers?

Who do your children like?

What do your children like?

Who do you like?

What do you like?

Once in Nigeria, I gathered the missionaries and I told them: « Even if you do not like me, even if you don't like our ministry, for God sake, succeed the missionary work you have started, so that you can show your success to your children." If you become a missionary and you fail, and you have nothing in you that you can boast about to your children, who will follow the failure of their parents?

I wanted the missionaries to succeed so as to offer their children something to admire. You can offer everything to your children and they will love you fondly. But in the presence of their friends, if they have nothing to be proud of, they will follow the friends who have something they are proud of.

A four-year-old boy was talking with his friends. One of the friends said: "My father has got a huge car called Cadillac. When you are inside, it is like a small heaven." Another said: "When my father sits in his office called the court, people fear him, and they bow to him. Each child was praising his father. Now, this young boy said: "My Dad is greater than all yours. Every Sunday, your parents come and sit in front of my dad and he talks to them, he shouts at them. I know only one person that my father fears. The person has a room in our house. I have never seen him. Whenever he enters that room to meet him, he locks the door. I kind of spy him, and I see my Dad on his knees, crying. My dad calls him 'My Lord Jesus', but also 'Heavenly Father'. My Dad fears him. My dad fears him. But my dad fears none of your fathers.

Children like boasting when they meet. This four-year-old kid was boasting. So, the boy's first knowledge of God was the One that his father feared. This boy became one of the greatest missionaries in our world, Adoniram Judson. Hallelujah!

What attracts us will produce admiration.

What we admire, we will imitate.

What we imitate will transform us.

The Lord Jesus had what attracted Him.

When I was small, there was a man in my father's village called John Mbande; I think he must have been a Jehovah Witness. He preached every day in the village, wearing clothes like John the Baptist. I still remember the song we composed about him in the dialect. We sang about John Mbande. But I never greeted him once in my whole life. I did not like him. I never listened to what John Mbande said. I do not remember giving him even one cup of water. I did not like meeting him on the road. I don't know how many years he preached. I don't know whether he made one convert.

But when I was going to school in a small town called Nkambe, there was a young Peace Corps lady, Miss Neil. I don't know whether that woman was preaching. Her house was about two or three kilometres from our house, far; but there is not a Sunday that we did not run to her house. Do you know why? She used to make some things that they called buns or scones. Buns, scones, biscuits, some fine small things and some nice sweets. I don't remember what Miss Neil said Jesus had done; but those biscuits, who can forget? Who can forget those scones? We went to Miss Neil's house, we never measured the distance, and I remember her name till today, a clean little white American who loved children. But she did something for us that helped me. She used to give us some booklets, "Our Daily Bread", and I read them. I read them.

Our mother was very strict. On Sunday, we had to wake up at the same time that we woke up when we went to school and we had to be in church at the same time that we got to school. So, at seven o'clock, we were dressed; only my brother and I we were in church, and we had to wait for two hours for the others to come, and that is the time I read my "Daily breads". I do not remember what I read; but just imagine a child, who at the age of nine, ten, read bible stories for two hours.

We could not play because our clothes were very clean; they were Sunday clothes. You could not play football with Sunday clothes. After two hours, our mother would have finished adult church, because in the Presbyterian church, there was what they called the order of service. She would sing the processional hymn which may be the Benedictus, then, she would do her first reading - it was posted there, from the Old Testament. And she would meditate, and sing the song, because the hymn is there. After that, she would do the second reading, from the New Testament. After the New Testament, she sang the hymn. For the sermon, she would be quiet and look over the passages that she read. After all that, she will sing the recession and go home. So, it is when she was going home that people were coming.

In Sunday school, we did not have an order of service; so, we had to wait for two hours, for other children to come. And that discipline made me study the Bible a lot. I read the "Daily bread", I read other Christian tracts, I read all Bible stories.

I liked Miss Neil, but from John Mbande, the preacher that went from quarter to quarter in the village, I don't remember anything. If we help the children like good people, God's people, you may not measure the impact that will follow them. And Miss Neil has left an impact on me till today. When children come to visit me, I don't want them to go back without one biscuit, because I still remember buns, scones, biscuits. And I read all the little pamphlets that she gave us.

3

TIMOTHY'S ADMIRATION

Timothy admired some people, and he was shaped by the people that he admired.

2 Timothy 3:10-15

[10]You, however, know all about my teaching, my way of life, my purpose, faith, patience, love, endurance, [11]persecutions, sufferings — what kinds of things happened to me in Antioch, Iconium and Lystra, the persecutions I endured. Yet the Lord rescued me from all of them. [12]In fact, everyone who wants to live a godly life in Christ Jesus will be persecuted, [13]while evil men and impostors will go from bad to worse, deceiving and being deceived. [14]But as for you, continue in what you have learned and have become convinced of, because you know those from whom you learned it, [15]and how from infancy you have known the holy Scriptures, which are able to make you wise for salvation through faith in Christ Jesus.

Timothy admired Paul and Paul knew that Timothy admired him. Paul was Timothy's university. Timothy noticed everything about Paul. He knew about Paul's goal, he knew about Paul's faith, he knew about Paul's love. He knew Paul's history. And Paul told him: continue in the teaching that you have received because you know and you admire those who taught you... Just like you know the Scriptures.

We find that like the Lord Jesus, Timothy had spiritual tendencies. He admired those who were serving God. He loved the Scriptures and He knew them, from when he was small. That is why we said that Timothy was apostle Paul's disciple. He put on the apostle Paul, because he imitated him, and he imitated him because he admired him.

Whom do you genuinely admire?

4

JOHN THE BAPTIST'S ADMIRATION

But there is one of the examples in the Bible that I really want us to look at. Do you know the person who has been the most shaped, transformed thanks to the person he admired? John the Baptist: even right in his mother's womb, when he entered the presence of Jesus, he danced with joy. Since the time he was yet in his mother's womb. When he grew up, he would see Jesus pass and tell his disciples: "Behold, the Lamb of God that takes away the sin of the world. He is the one I told you about. He does not baptise with water; he baptises men with the Holy Spirit. For the Father gave us the Spirit by measure, according to our needs; but to Him, God gave the fullness of the Holy Spirit. He is the one I told you about; I am not even worthy to untie the thongs of His sandals. He was there the next day, and when Jesus came by, he said: "Behold, the Lamb of God!" From his mother's womb to his thirties, each time he saw Jesus, he had some praise for Him. He was always praising Jesus, always worshipping Jesus.

And you see, even unconsciously, he eventually became like Jesus? Concerning Jesus' inner life, the Bible says that though He was equal to God, He made Himself nothing. Later on, John the Baptist tells his disciples: "You don't know Him. No man is His equal. He must become greater; I must become less. He must become greater and greater, while I become smaller and smaller."

And We Know that John's life was marked with humility. The man Jesus described John as the greatest man born of a woman. He put on Jesus in His humility and self-renunciation. He was fascinated, he imitated, he was transformed, he put on Jesus in His humility and self-renunciation. He was captivated, he admired, he imitated, and he was transformed. Glory to God ! Transformed by His admiration.

So, right from the mother's womb, it is possible to be fascinated by certain people. It is possible to start admiring some people that come to the mother's environment. You don't know why you love series that much; that is what your mother did when you were in her womb. While your mother was pregnant, she was told to stay away from church for forty days after child birth. To stay forty days away from the presence of God... So, for the first four days of your life, you were separated from God, and now your face is dark. When they talk about God, you wonder why they are disturbing people. Ask your mother why she spent 40 days away from Church?

Right from his mother's womb, John the Baptist 'leaped with joy' when he got into the presence of Jesus. And right to the end of his life, in prison, He was asking Jesus questions. What many have failed to notice is that John's thoughts were all turned to Jesus. He had no food, no clothes, no friends, no wife, no children, no house, no car, no farm. But when John saw Jesus, he leapt with joy. Even as a grown-up, when he saw Jesus, he would speak: "It is him I told you about. Now you see him! You see him!" Clap for John!

The unique thing about John was not his lacks, but his admiration. He admired Jesus, He loved Jesus. He explained Jesus. He sent men to Jesus. He lost his ministry because of Jesus. In the case of Jesus, He obtained what he admired: His Father's presence. Timothy admired Paul so deeply. John the Baptist admired the Lord Jesus so much that he ended up being like Jesus, profoundly humble. That which captivates us, we shall admire. That which we admire, we shall imitate. That which we imitate, we shall become. It was true with Jesus. It was true with Timothy. And John the Baptist is a clear illustration.

What are the spiritual impulses of your heart? What are the spiritual inclinations of your heart? What have you got affectionate to? What is there in your heart for God, for which no one needs to force you? What is that which brings you joy? When David says:

> *"Even the sparrow has found a home, and the swallow a nest for herself, where she may have her young — a place near your altar, O Lord Almighty, my King and my God [...] Better is one day in your courts than a thousand elsewhere"* (Ps 84:3-4, 10)

Why there? What is there that you love as much as this? Is there anything you admire like this?

You cannot produce disciples without helping them love good men, the men of the Bible, God's things. And this flows from the people we expose the children to. If these people are frustrated parents, all the teaching they may receive will not correct what they have seen.

> *Pray that God gives us many "John the Baptist", so attracted to Jesus, that many of the things that all of us are running after will mean nothing to them.*

Like Jesus, like Timothy, like John the Baptist, what we admire, we will become. Brother Alphonse wants to give us a summary.

A recap from brother Alphonse Tawet

Praise the Lord!

We are going to read the example of John the Baptist who was captivated by the Lord Jesus, who imitated the Lord Jesus and who became like the Lord Jesus. We shall read a few Bible passages.

John the Baptist, captivated by the Lord Jesus

Luke 1:39-44.

39 At that time Mary got ready and hurried to a town in the hill country of Judea, 40 where she entered Zechariah's home and greeted Elizabeth. 41 When Elizabeth heard Mary's greeting, the baby leapt in her womb, and Elizabeth was filled with the Holy Spirit. 42 In a loud voice she exclaimed: "Blessed are you among women, and blessed is the child you will bear! 43 But why am I so favoured, that the mother of my Lord should come to me? 44 As soon as the sound of your greeting reached my ears, the baby in my womb leapt for joy.

The child who leapt for joy was John the Baptist, captivated from his mother's womb.

John 1:24-27

^{24}Now some Pharisees who had been sent ^{25}questioned him, "Why then do you baptize if you are not the Christ, nor Elijah, nor the Prophet?" ^{26}"I baptise with water," John replied, "but among you stands one you do not know. ^{27}He is the one who comes after me, the thongs of whose sandals I am not worthy to untie."

John the Baptist admires Jesus.

John 1:29-36

^{29}The next day John saw Jesus coming toward him and said, "Look, the Lamb of God, who takes away the sin of the world! ^{30}This is the one I meant when I said, 'A man who comes after me has surpassed me because he was before me.' ^{31}I myself did not know him, but the reason I came baptising with water was that he might be revealed to Israel." ^{32}Then John gave this testimony: "I saw the Spirit come down from heaven as a dove and remains on him. ^{33}I would not have known him, except that the one who sent me to baptize with water told me, 'The man on whom you see the Spirit come down and remain is he who will baptize with the Holy Spirit.' ^{34}I have seen and I testify that this is the Son of God." ^{35}The next day John was there again with two of his disciples. When he saw Jesus passing by, he said, "Look, the Lamb of God!"

John the Baptist imitates Jesus

Humble, like the Master

John 3:26-32

^{26}They came to John and said to him, "Rabbi, that man who was with you on the other side of the Jordan — the one you testified about — well, he is baptising, and everyone is going to him." ^{27}To this John replied, "A man can receive only what is given him from heaven. ^{28}You yourselves can testify that I said, 'I am not the Christ but am sent ahead of him.' ^{29}The bride belongs to the bridegroom. The friend who attends the bridegroom waits and listens for him, and is full of joy when he hears the bridegroom's voice. That joy is mine, and it is now complete. ^{30}He must become greater; I must become less. ^{31}"The one who comes from above is above all; the one who is from the earth belongs to the earth, and speaks as one from the earth. The one who comes from heaven is above all.

He died like the Master

Matt 14:9-12

^{9}The king was distressed, but because of his oaths and his dinner guests, he ordered that her request be granted ^{10}and had John beheaded in the prison. ^{11}His head was brought in on a platter and given to the girl, who carried it to her mother. ^{12}John's disciples came and took his body and buried it. Then they went and told Jesus.

He owned nothing, like the Master

Mark 1:6

John wore clothing made of camel's hair, with a leather belt around his waist, and he ate locusts and wild honey.

John the Baptist became like Jesus.

The testimony of the Lord Jesus Himself about John

Matt 11:11

I tell you the truth: Among those born of women there has not risen anyone greater than John the Baptist...

The testimony of Herod

Matt 14:1-2

[1]At that time Herod the tetrarch heard the reports about Jesus, [2]and he said to his attendants, "This is John the Baptist; he has risen from the dead! That is why miraculous powers are at work in him."

John was so transformed into the like of Jesus that wicked Herod thought Jesus equals to John. John was captivated by Jesus, he admired Jesus, he imitated Jesus, and he was transformed.

Praise the Lord!

What are you attracted to?

Whom are you attracted to?

The Lord Jesus loved the presence of God, the young Timothy loved and admired the apostle, Paul.

We disciple our children by shaping their attractions, not by imposing it, even though there are some that we need to impose, because they are so many sons of Belial, that we must first cast out Belial out of them, and the instrument that cast out Belial is "Doctor do good". There are many children who just love evil. When they are in a group, they want to pinch somebody.

The Lord Jesus enjoyed the presence of God so much that the only time in His life, when He ran away from His parents, it was to go into the presence of God.

As we lead children to God, after praying with a child and Jesus enters his heart, you are to study to see the spiritual tilts of that child's life. If new appetites do not enter that child's life... When someone believes in the Lord Jesus, even before a change in his character, new tilts and new desires possess them.

Next, we shall look at the children who admired Jesus to the point of celebrating Him, the children who were in the crowd to welcome Jesus to Jerusalem. In those days, when the people said: Hosanna to the Son of David, the clergy did nothing. But when those children started worshipping Jesus, when they started singing the same thing (Those children had seen the disciples worship and adore Jesus, and, in turn, they admired Jesus), the clergy almost died. They told Jesus: "Tell the children to keep quiet". And Jesus replied: "If they keep quiet, the stones will cry out."

When the children are amidst the worshippers of Jesus, they are trained to admire Jesus. This is what we shall cover next. We shall study the choir of the children who adore Jesus. The grown-ups worship Jesus, but the children too should worship Jesus. And when it is the children that worship Jesus... the children cast out demons more than the older people, because the Bible says:

"From the lips of children and infants you have ordained praise because of your enemies, to silence the foe and the avenger." (Ps 8:2)

Last year, we wanted <u>children who are champions</u>. This year, we want <u>children who are worshippers</u>. We do not mean those who sing with a beautiful voice, but worshippers, those who admire the Lord Jesus as they have seen the older people do.

When you admire Jesus, you will sing Jesus!

When you welcome Jesus, you will sing Jesus!!

When you receive Jesus, you will sing Jesus!!!

We do not only have the examples of Jesus who was fond of the presence of God or Timothy who admired Paul. There were many other children who admired Jesus, who came to welcome Jesus, sing Jesus, celebrate Jesus, dance Jesus. And when children begin to worship Jesus, Satan's works crumble.

Children who are champions!

Children who are worshippers!!

Children who are praisers!!!

Hallelujah!!!!

That is what we shall study next. And I shall give you an assignment: that each one of you come to this course next year with the song he will have written for the Lord Jesus that he admires.

CRAFTING A CHILD'S ADMIRATIONS

The things that you admire now is what you will become later on. What you admire now, you will become later. If you admire worldly people, worldly musicians, worldly politicians, worldly artists, that is what you will become in a few years. What you admire, you become. What you see a lot and admire a lot, you will become. Even animals are like that.

Jacob, the son of Isaac, practised some witchcraft on Laban's sheep. What was the sorcery? What was the witchcraft? He knew that what the animals see when they are mating is what they will give birth to. So, he peeled poplar plants and put them in front of the animals: white, brown, white, brown, white, brown, so that when they are mating, they will see those lines. What you admire today is what you will become tomorrow. And, something happened: when the sheep delivered, all the young had lines, or dots.

What you admire, you become. What you see, you become. What you concentrate on, you shall become.

Pray that you will select to admire what you
will become.

THEY BECOME WHAT THEY SEE AND LISTENS TO

I did not understand many things in the past. Our elder
brother with whom we grew for some time was very choosy
about the kind of music we listened to, about the places we
went to, even about the books that we read. He limited our
listening to Cameroonian musicians only to two, because, as
he explained, the others were only making noise. I think
since he was a Presbyterian, he told us to listen to Eboa
Lotin. So, in the house, the only Cameroon musician you will
find was Eboa Lotin who played very simply. He allowed us
to listen to Manu Dibango, because he said his music was at
least, a form of art and perfection in the music. He added a
third one later on: Francis Bebey. Those were the only
Cameroonian musicians we were permitted to listen to. He
bought the music that he wanted us to listen to, and he
banned us from going to cinema, even though we cheated
and went without his knowing. Our elder brother selected
what we saw, what we listened to, and the places we went to.

For our outings, he used to arrange which family we will visit.
We were not allowed to go anywhere. He did not stop us
from going out, but he selected where we went. What you
see and you admire, you shall become. What you listen to,
what you enjoy is what you will like, what you will become.

When Brother Zach took me to India, I met an evangelist
there, a very humble man. He invited Brother Zach for a
meal and we went along with Brother Zach. He had very
unusual spiritual gifts. I was touched because, he said he had
the gift of the word of knowledge. He said: "To my right,

there is lady that has a cancer". Somebody stood up. He said: "No, you are not the one." Then he kept looking, he counted the benches. He said: "You are on the 32nd bench, towards the window, Jesus is healing you, stand up!" He saw clearly in the spirit; he was not guessing. He would not talk and then expect that somebody help him accomplish his prophecy.

He invited Brother Zach to his house, and he told Brother Zach that his mother-in-law was sick. He said he is an evangelist with the gift of healing, but he does not have faith to heal his mother-in-law, but that Brother Zach should pray for his mother-in-law. First of all, I was touched by his honesty.

After Brother Zach prayed and the mother -in-law was healed, Bother Zach asked him: "What is the secret to your life." He said when he was very small, his father was a very poor missionary, but that many pastors came to their house. When these pastors came, he would wash their shoes, polish them, iron their clothes, get them towels. As those pastors were leaving, many of them did not have any money. So, they would call him, put their hands on him and bless him. He said, they kept blessing him like that. He said that one day, around when he was fourteen, his eyes opened in the spiritual such that he could see in the spiritual as clearly as he saw in the natural, and it continued. He said he did not remember when it happened, but that maybe hundreds of pastors had blessed him. He had served those pastors that passed through his father's house, and they blessed him. And he was then a big evangelist, maybe India's biggest evangelist, with a very massive headquarters.

I had met him earlier on before he invited Brother Zach. When we had finished preaching in Bangalore, there were so many people who wanted to see Brother Zach. A very young and handsome man came to me and said: "Theodore, please, I would like to ask you certain things"; He called me aside and he said: "Tell me a bit about Brother Zach!" I shared a little. I didn't know he was the big evangelist that we would meet in the evening. So, when we met in the evening, he looked at me, he was laughing. So, I asked him: "Why did you come to me, everybody goes to the preacher, why did you come to me?" He told me that he knows that people don't notice servants though they are the ones who know their master, and that he was truly interested in Brother Zach. He said: "Don't you see? everybody went to Brother Zach; I've had a long time to talk with you. So, I now know Brother Zach more than all those people who went to him [...] I came to you because I am like you. I grew up knowing how to be a servant and all the gifts I have, I received them because I was a servant."

The lesson I want us to learn from that evangelist is that the people you expose your children to are the people you have decided that your children will take after. The father allowed him, exposed him to missionaries, and he became a great evangelist. We have to be very careful about the people we expose our children to, those we send our children on holidays to, because they will become like the people that they admire, and the things you expose your children to are what they will end up loving.

I know a brother, a very wonderful brother. In his childhood, the mother was a prostitute in Douala. She used to bring the men to their house. So, he told me it used to pain him to see so many men coming to sleep with his mother but that, after sometimes, he started going to watch them. Later on, he became a believer, a very loving brother. But after he married, he drove his wife. The wife did not know what she had done. When the wife wanted to come near him, he drove her. The wife complained to me. I called the brother and asked him why. He told me that his wife did not love him. I said: "What? Everybody knows that your wife loves you!" Later on he confessed; he told me: "When I am sleeping with her, she does not make noise the way my mother used to make with those men." Can you image the kind of things that had stained his head? So, no matter what the wife did, what remained in his head was how a prostitute behaves, because that is what he watched. He had been corrupted, corrupted. It took me long to convince him that his mother did not love those men.

We should watch out what we expose our children to, the people we bring into their lives, because they will become like them, morally corrupt or morally excellent. Part of the ministry to children is to offer the children models.

One of our biggest ministries to children is this "Instant ZTF". If we give the children somebody to admire, we have radically changed them. What they admire, they will become. What they admire, they will imitate. What they admire will transform them. One of the missionary couples in Nigeria is doing what Sister Henriette does in "Instant ZTF". They are doing it in a bigger way: they go to a secondary school and ask the principal for permission, and they shared about Brother Zach, from the book *From His Lips*, all the teachers then want to buy the book. And the principal keeps inviting them, they have many schools that want them to come and share.

What we admire, we shall become!

What we admire, we shall become!!

CULTIVATING GOOD VALUES AND ENTERTAINMENTS

When I was thirteen, I went on holidays to Yaoundé, at Prof Moukake's house, because my brother-in-law was there. There was a big shop called "Monoprix". They used to sell yoghurt, half a litre, one litre. When you settled on that yoghurt, you knew what enjoyment feels like. So, my brother-in-law gave me a book, a big book. The title was *A Walk in the Night,* by Alex La Gouma, a South African writer. It was one of the books in the African series. He told me: "If you finish reading this book and give me a summary, I will buy you a litre of yoghurt." I tell you, my eyes were on that litre of yoghurt. I think in less than two days, when he came back from work, I rapidly gave him a summary, because I had a magnetic memory. The next day, he came home with my litre of yoghurt. I ate that yoghurt. But my brother-in-law had done something to me that has lasted till today: the capacity to read much, fast, and remember. From that time, even without the yoghurt, I read a lot and I remembered.

What we expose the children to, to be wonderful, they will remember, they will remember. In our ministry to children, in our love for children, we should expose them to good people and to good habits. We should cultivate their values and we should cultivate their entertainments.

My wife was surprised when we got married. After some time, she told me that she is my second wife. I was surprised! I asked her: "With whom did you catch me?" She replied: "Your first wife is books, and I am your second wife." Because after a long day, when I wanted to relax, I read. So, she asked me how somebody can relax by reading. For her, reading is work. How can you relax by reading? But my brother-in-law had made reading a pleasure. He had given me something that I could do, that would not tax me.

EXPOSURE TO GOOD PEOPLE AND GOOD HABITS

Matt 19:13-15

Then little children were brought to Jesus for him to place his hands on them and pray for them. But the disciples rebuked those who brought them. [14]Jesus said, "Let the little children come to me, and do not hinder them, for the kingdom of heaven belongs to such as these." [15]When he had placed his hands on them, he went on from there.

Mark 10:13-16

[13]People were bringing little children to Jesus to have him touch them, but the disciples rebuked them. [14]When Jesus saw this, he was indignant. He said to them, "Let the little children come to me, and do not hinder them, for the kingdom of God belongs to such as these. [15]I tell you the truth, anyone who will not receive the kingdom of God like a little child will never enter it." [16]And he took the children in his arms, put his hands on them and blessed them.

Luke 18:15-17

[15]People were also bringing babies to Jesus to have him touch them. When the disciples saw this, they rebuked them. [16]But Jesus called the children to him and said, "Let the little children come to me, and do not hinder them, for the kingdom of God belongs to such as these. [17]I tell you the truth, anyone who will not receive the kingdom of God like a little child will never enter it."

These parents knew what is important. They exposed their children to the Lord Jesus. The children were not sick, the children were not poor. They did not bring the children so that the children should have something worldly or material but they wanted to expose the children to the influence of Jesus. They just wanted Jesus to touch them, because the children would remember it. There was something in Jesus' touch, in Jesus' laying of hands, in Jesus' blessing, in the love of Jesus, in the tenderness of Jesus, that would mark the children. They were wise.

Even in our families, we ought to invite and expose our children to those who are noble, to those who will love them, to those who will bless them. In school, we ought to look out for some teachers that love our children, that will bless them.

I was blessed with many good teachers. In primary six, I came from the village. We had an English teacher called Mr Ndip. He was a vain man, but he liked me. And at that time in Buea, there was a radio programme called: "Quiz for schools". Even though I came from the village, they selected intelligent children to represent the school. All of us went to the radio programme and we formed camps in the studio. It was a woman who used to interview us. There were about thirty questions. She would start from A; if you don't answer, they go to B, the other school. And the school that answers more questions than the other one has won. So, it was an intellectual match.

Mr Ndip insisted that they should put me. The other children were still laughing at me. In those days, they used to call those who come from the village CFC ('Come from country'), 'Just come from country', 'Johnny just come'. The other students were still laughing at me like CFC when Mr Ndip insisted that I should go. And since I used to read wildly, I became like a small champion in our group, and we won many matches. But he helped me. He helped me in general knowledge.

I also had a maths teacher called Mr Wallang. The man just liked me. After school, he used to take me home to eat. From that day, my normal mark in mathematics was 100%; because I was not seeing maths again, it was Mr Wallang. All of you sitting here prove that if you like a teacher, you will pass his subject. All of you. If you just like a teacher, his subject becomes easy. Mr Wallang made mathematics as enjoyable as the beans that he carried me to eat at his house. When you are sending a child to school, pray that some good teacher will like your child, it will change everything. What we admire, we shall become. You surely remember your own case as I talk, and you know it at home, among your relatives, at school, even in the church.

I met a grown-up sister not long ago, when she was small, she called me and asked me: Uncle, am I still a virgin? I asked her what happened. She said: "Many pastors come to our house and one of those uncles was holding me and put his finger in me. Am I still a virgin?" I was so wounded when she told me that it was when she was small. All I told her was, "Forgive that 'Tonton'." A pastor comes home and it is the pastor that destroys your child!!! So, even in the church, you should be honest in selecting good people to whom your children associate. Because even in the church, there are some demons that destroy people.

The people who brought children to Jesus, to expose them to Jesus so Jesus could touch them, so Jesus could bless them, so

Jesus could embrace them, were actually ministering to the children. The touch, the embrace, the blessing of a man who carries God, who carries the presence of God, of a man who carries the holiness of God, can produce in a child an inner feeling of that which is excellent and heavenly. It can remodel the inner dispositions of the child. So, part of our ministry to children is to select, as ministers to children, good people, good influences, good people who are full of God.

MOULDING THROUGH CELEBRATIONS AND FESTIVALS

Matt 21:6-16

[6]The disciples went and did as Jesus had instructed them. [7]They brought the donkey and the colt, placed their cloaks on them, and Jesus sat on them. [8]A very large crowd spread their cloaks on the road, while others cut branches from the trees and spread them on the road. [9]The crowds that went ahead of him and those that followed shouted, "Hosanna to the Son of David!" "Blessed is he who comes in the name of the Lord!" "Hosanna in the highest!" [10]When Jesus entered Jerusalem, the whole city was stirred and asked, "Who is this?" [11]The crowds answered, "This is Jesus, the prophet from Nazareth in Galilee."

[12]Jesus entered the temple area and drove out all who were buying and selling there. He overturned the tables of the money changers and the benches of those selling doves. [13]"It is written," he said to them, "'My house will be called a house of prayer,' but you are making it a 'den of robbers.'" [14]The blind and the lame came to him at the temple, and he healed them. [15]But when the chief priests and the teachers of the law saw the wonderful things he did and the children shouting in the temple area, "Hosanna to the Son of

David," they were indignant. [16]"Do you hear what these children are saying?" they asked him. "Yes," replied Jesus, "have you never read, "'From the lips of children and infants you have ordained praise'?"

There was a great event: Jesus was entering Jerusalem. The disciples of Jesus prepared for that mega church service. They decorated the road with palm trees, it was a high day, and then the Lord Jesus came. And then the whole crowd, with the disciples, were shouting: "Hosanna to the Son of David. Blessed is he that comes in the Name of the Lord, Hosanna in the Highest." It was a hymn, they were singing, shouting, proclaiming. And the children who came along they caught it, they caught the event. And they too started worshipping Jesus, the way they saw the older people do. They too started shouting: Hosanna to the Son of David. From the older people, they learnt a song of praise and they started singing it. There is a difference.

On the day of the triumphal entry, the children were there. After the old people went home, the children continued following Jesus. When he went to the temple, they followed Him. So, the children started disturbing the high priests, because every day, when Jesus came to the temple, there was the crowd of children that followed Him and shouted, like that first day: "Hosanna to the Son of David!" What the children catch, they keep repeating. Even when the older people had stopped. They were the ones following Jesus now. Every day, Jesus went to the temple and they would shout and praise Him.

The final choir that accompanied Jesus at the end of His life, to the cross, was the choir of the children. The choir at the beginning was the choir of angels, but at the end, it was the choir of the children. The Lord Jesus started His ministry with the choir of the angels when He was born, and at the end, when He came to Jerusalem to die, He was accompanied by the choir of children. When Jesus was going to the cross, He went to war with the devil, the choir of warfare of Jesus was the company and the proclamations of the children: "Hosanna to the Son of David". Which actually means: "The Son of David is the Saviour". Hosanna means "Oh! Save, save, Saviour". The final choir in the work of Jesus, accompanying the Son of David to be the Saviour of the world was the choir of the children.

There are two lessons. The first is our need for festivals, our need for praise festivals. The disciples had a praise festival to accompany Jesus into Jerusalem. They had a praise festival, a celebration event. We need our events, where we shall praise God, so that it leaves an impact on the children. Festivals, celebrations, events of worship are a way of transforming children. Children are marked by celebrations. Children are marked by celebrations.

In the village, Christmas day was wonderful. On Christmas day, all of us children, with our friends, on that day, we will go together to this one's house and they bring out his Christmas food and we ate together. Then we move from there, to the next person's house, and they bring out his food, and we ate it. We were to go round like that until we finish all who were in our group.

There is one Christmas day that I cannot forget because I regretted very much. That day, we started in our house. We had cooked pork. I did not know that pork fills the stomach, and I ate, especially the fatty parts. We ate. After that, my stomach was standing like a mortar. When we went to the next house, I could no longer eat. That Christmas day, we covered all the houses and my stomach did not go down, it was just standing there like that, like a stone. So, that was the only thing I ate that day, and that is the only Christmas I remember in details, because that pork made my Christmas day miserable.

Events mark children.

Worship marks children.

We have seen that at the level of the family, we should expose our children to people who can impact them. But at the level of the church, we are to have events, celebrations, festivals of praise, to mark our children. We are to have praise and we are to involve the children.

In great celebrations, Jesus is revealed to the children through the songs we sing, and the enjoyment that they see us having in Jesus. They will be impacted by the great celebrations, and Jesus will be revealed to them when they see our enjoyment in Him. In turn, they shall worship the One for whom their parents sing.

At the level of the home, let us bring them to Jesus, let us expose them to men of godliness. And at the level of the church, please let's have events, celebrations, festivals full of praise, so that our children may know God.

There are nations that have their events, today, is one of the events of Cameroon, the Youth Day. And the children prepare, and they are influenced, they are impacted. Every nation highlights their values by celebrations, by holidays.

The people of God, the disciples of Christ should have the great events of the Lord and celebrate them: in the breaking of bread, in praise, in worship, and the children are to be involved. Worship, praise is commutative.

Even in the world, many great musicians of the world were produced in the church praise: Michael Jackson used to sing in the church, in the choir. Beyonce sang in the church. Elvis Presley sang in the church, Manu Dibango sang in the church. R. Kelly sang in the church. Many big musicians in the world were influenced by praise in the church. They did not have Jesus, but the songs and the celebration fell on them.

Nations celebrate their values by festivals. The church ought to celebrate Jesus, and our children will be influenced, and God will rise among us.

Even in the church in Yaoundé, most of our musicians learnt music in the church. It is our praise, our celebrations, our worship that will leave the most permanent mark on our children, and if our worship is full of Jesus and if Jesus is in our worship, our children will know Him and they will worship Him as they saw us worship Him. We must have events, meetings, occasions, festivals at the level of the local church, at the level of the ministry, so that our children may know God.

Rev. Chillhead was a missionary in the Basel Mission, who used to visit Brother Zach's father. He was a very unusual man. He was like the disciple maker of Brother Zach's father. And every time he came home, they will clean the whole compound, and he will stay in the office with Brother Zach's father and pray with him, and they will share. Ma Hodia told me that none of them would dare to make noise on that day. He was a man of unusual holiness.

And when Brother Zach was about eight years old, that man came to their family, and after finishing with Brother Zach's father, he told Brother Zach's father: "I will soon be going back to Switzerland. Give me one of your children to bless." Brother Zach was brought to him and that man blessed Brother Zach, blessed Brother Zach. That is why, even before believing, he became like different from his other brothers. The missionary was called, he was an unusual holy man, and he took God seriously. I think he impacted to Brother Zach that hunger for God that characterised him.

The people we expose our children to and the events that we celebrate will mark our children. If there are pastors here, maybe we are not going to celebrate Palm Sundays, but let us have our events in which we celebrate Jesus in sincerity, where we worship the Lord, and, let us raise a choir of children. Their praise of Jesus will be free from the terrible corruption of the love of glory and the impact on the devil will be devastating.

> Pray that we learn from the Bible to raise a
> choir of children who will sing the songs
> we sing, with greater spiritual impact,
> because their hearts are free from the
> desire of fame, that fills many of the bigger
> ministers.

> Pray that God will give us children who are
> praise ministers, that love Jesus, that sing
> for Jesus.

BACK MATTERS

VERY IMPORTANT!!!

If you have not yet received Jesus as your Lord and Saviour, I encourage you to receive Him. Here are some steps to help you,

ADMIT that you are a sinner by nature and by practice and that on your own you are without hope. Tell God you have personally sinned against Him in your thoughts, words and deeds. Confess your sins to Him, one after another in a sincere prayer. Do not leave out any sins that you can remember. Truly turn from your sinful ways and abandon them. If you stole, steal no more. If you have been committing adultery or fornication, stop it. God will not forgive you if you have no desire to stop sinning in all areas of your life, but if you are sincere, He will give you the power to stop sinning.

BELIEVE that Jesus Christ, who is God's Son, is the only Way, the only Truth and the only Life. Jesus said,

"I am the way, the truth and the life; no one comes to the Father, but by me" (John 14:6).

The Bible says,

"For there is one God, and there is one mediator between God and men, the man Christ Jesus, who gave himself as a ransom for all" (1 Timothy 2:5-6).

"And there is salvation in no one else (apart from Jesus), for there is no other name under heaven given among men by which we must be saved" (Acts 4:12).

But to all who received him, who believed in his name, he gave power to become children of God..." (John 1:12).

BUT,

CONSIDER the cost of following Him. Jesus said that all who follow Him must deny themselves, and this includes selfish financial, social and other interests. He also wants His followers to take up their crosses and follow Him. Are you prepared to abandon your own interests daily for those of Christ? Are you prepared to be led in a new direction by Him? Are you prepared to suffer for Him and die for Him if need be? Jesus will have nothing to do with half-hearted people. His demands are total. He will only receive and forgive those who are prepared to follow Him AT ANY COST. Think about it and count the cost. If you are prepared to follow Him, come what may, then there is something to do.

INVITE Jesus to come into your heart and life. He says,

"Behold I stand at the door and knock. If anyone hears my voice and opens the door (to his heart and life), I will come in to him and eat with him, and he with me" (Revelation 3:20).

Why don't you pray a prayer like the following one or one of your own construction as the Holy Spirit leads?

> "Lord Jesus, I am a wretched, lost sinner who
> has sinned in thought, word and deed.
> Forgive all my sins and cleanse me. Receive
> me, Saviour and transform me into a child
> of God. Come into my heart now and give
> me eternal life right now. I will follow you
> at all costs, trusting the Holy Spirit to give
> me all the power I need."

When you pray this prayer sincerely, Jesus answers at once and justifies you before God and makes you His child.

*Please write to us (**ztfbooks@cmfionline.org**) and I will pray for you and help you as you go on with Jesus Christ.*

God has tied the salvation of the world to a child—Jesus—who was born in a stable. **Children are a sacred trust given by God.** Bringing up the future generation is

- the highest,
- the holiest, and
- the noblest

calling one could ever have. This responsibility falls on parents as well as ministers to children.

This book is a plea from Professor *Zacharias Tanee Fomum* who had an intense burden for the salvation of children, given that he himself had given his life to the Lord Jesus at the age of 11.

From Bible examples such as Isaac, Samuel, John the Baptist, and the Lord Jesus Himself, Professor *Fomum* proves that it is possible to come to Jesus, know and serve Him early in life and that the consecration of a child to God paves the way for him to follow, from which he will not depart.

This book is a must-read for every godly parent and minister to children.

RECOMMENDED BOOKS

https://ztfbooks.com

THE CHRISTIAN WAY

1. The Way Of Life
2. The Way Of Obedience
3. The Way Of Discipleship
4. The Way Of Sanctification
5. The Way Of Christian Character
6. The Way Of Spiritual Power
7. The Way Of Christian Service
8. The Way Of Spiritual Warfare
9. The Way Of Suffering For Christ
10. The Way Of Victorious Praying
11. The Way Of Overcomers
12. The Way Of Spiritual Encouragement
13. The Way Of Loving The Lord

THE PRAYER POWER SERIES

1. The Way Of Victorious Praying
2. The Ministry Of Fasting
3. The Art Of Intercession
4. The Practice Of Intercession
5. Praying With Power
6. Practical Spiritual Warfare Through Prayer
7. Moving God Through Prayer
8. The Ministry Of Praise And Thanksgiving
9. Waiting On The Lord In Prayer

PRACTICAL HELPS FOR OVERCOMERS

LEADING GOD'S PEOPLE

GOD, SEX AND YOU

OFF-SERIES

THE SPIRIT-FILLED LIFE

GOD, MONEY AND YOU

PRACTICAL HELPS IN SANCTIFICATION

MAKING SPIRITUAL PROGRESS

EVANGELISM

1. 36 Reasons For Winning The Lost To Christ
2. Soul Winning, Volume 1
3. Soul Winning, Volume 2
4. The Winning of The Lost as Life's Supreme Task
5. Salvation And Soul-Winning
6. Soul Winning And The Making Of Disciples
7. <u>Victorious Soul-Winning</u>

GOD LOVES YOU

1. God's Love And Forgiveness
2. The Way Of Life
3. Come Back Home My Son; I Still Love You
4. Celebrity A Mask
5. Encounter The Saviour
6. Meet The Liberator
7. Jesus is The Answer

JESUS STILL HEALS TODAY

1. Jesus Loves You And Wants To Heal You
2. Come And See; Jesus Has Not Changed!
3. Jesus Saves And Heals Today
4. Miracles, Healings, and Deliverances

WOMEN OF THE GLORY

1. The Secluded Worshipper: Prophetess Anna
2. Unending Intimacy: Mary of Bethany

3. Winning Love: Mary Magdalene

ANTHOLOGIES

1. The School of Soul Winners and Soul Winning
2. The Complete Works of Z.T.F on Holiness (Volume 1)
3. The Complete Works of Z.T.F on Basic Christian Doctrine
4. The Complete Works of Z.T.F on Marriage (Volume 1)
5. The Complete Works of Z.T.F on The Gospel Message (Volume 1)
6. The Complete Works of Z.T.F on Prayer (Volume 1)
7. The Complete Works of Z.T.F on Prayer (Volume 2)
8. The Complete Works of Z.T.F on Prayer (Volume 3)
9. The Complete Works of Z.T.F on Prayer (Volume 4)
10. The Complete Works of Z.T.F on Prayer (Volume 5)
11. The Complete Works of Z.T.F on Leadership (Volume 1)
12. The Complete Works of Z.T.F on Leadership (Volume 2)
13. The Complete Works of Z.T.F on Leadership (Volume 3)
14. The Complete Works of Z.T. F on Leadership (Vol 4)

SPECIAL SERIES

1. A Broken Vessel
2. The Joy of Begging to Belong to the Lord Jesus Christ: A Testimony

3. Separation from the common
4. My Separation from the Common unto God and World Conquest

AUTO-BIOGRAPHICAL SERIES

1. From His Lips: About The Author
2. From His Lips: About His Co-Workers
3. From His Lips: Back From His Missions
4. From His Lips: About Our Ministry
5. From His Lips: On Our Vision
6. From His Lips: The work is the worker
7. From His Lips: The Battles He Fought
8. From His Lips: The Authority And Power of His Life
9. From His Lips: The Influences That Moulded Him: People And Books
10. From His Lips: The story of his life of seeking God
11. From His Lips: The facets of his ministry
12. From His Lips: The fruit of his life
13. From His Lips: The Movements He Birthed

THE OVERTHROW OF PRINCIPALITIES

1. Deliverance From Demons
2. The Prophecy Of The Overthrow Of The Satanic Prince Of Cameroon
3. The Prophecy of the Overthrow of The Satanic Prince of Yaounde
4. The Prophecy of the Overthrow of The Satanic Prince of Douala
5. The overthrow of principalities and powers

6. From His Lips: The Battles He Fought

OTHER BOOKS

1. The Missionary as a Son
2. What Our Ministry is
3. Conserver la Moisson
4. Disciples of Jesus Christ to Make Disciples For Jesus Christ
5. The House Church in God's Eternal Purposes
6. Christian Maturation
7. Heroes of the Kingdom
8. Spiritual Leadership in the Pattern of Gideon
9. The School of Evangelism
10. A Good Minister of Jesus Christ
11. Building a Spiritual Nation: The Foundation
12. Building a Spiritual Nation: Spiritual Statesmanship
13. Watching in Prayer
14. The Character of the Christian Worker
15. Church and Mission
16. Strategic Missionary Work
17. The Power of Brokenness
18. Growing with the Work
19. Blessing for growth

PRAISE, PRAYER AND FASTING CRUSADES

1. The Chronicles of Our Ministry [PFC2017]
2. Preparing to Encounter God [PFC2019]
3. The Making of Disciples: The Master's Way [PFC2020]

OUR DISTRIBUTORS

These books can be obtained in French and English Language from any of the following distribution outlets:

EDITIONS DU LIVRE CHRETIEN (ELC)

- **Location:** Paris, France
- **Email:** editionlivrechretien@gmail.com
- **Phone:** +33 6 98 00 90 47

INTERNET

- **Location:** on all major online **eBook, Audiobook** and **print-on-demand** (paperback) retailers.
- **Email**: ztfbooks@cmfionline.org
- **Phone**: +47 454 12 804
- **Website**: ztfbooks.com

CPH YAOUNDE

- **Location:** Yaounde, Cameroon
- **Email:** editionsztf@gmail.com
- **Phone:** +237 74756559

ZTF LITERATURE AND MEDIA HOUSE

- **Location:** Lagos, Nigeria
- **Email:** zlmh@ztfministry.org
- **Phone:** +2348152163063

CPH BURUNDI

- **Location:** Bujumbura, Burundi
- **Email:** cph-burundi@ztfministry.org
- **Phone:** +257 79 97 72 75

CPH UGANDA

- **Location:** Kampala, Uganda
- **Email:** cph-uganda@ztfministry.org
- **Phone:** +256 785 619613

CPH SOUTH AFRICA

- **Location:** Johannesburg, RSA
- **Email:** tantohtantoh@yahoo.com
- **Phone:** +27 83 744 5682